MY AUTOBIOGRAPHY
SEASONED BY STRESS

MY AUTOBIOGRAPHY
SEASONED BY STRESS

MARCO TORAL

LitPrime Solutions
21250 Hawthorne Blvd
Suite 500, Torrance, CA 90503
www.litprime.com
Phone: 1-800-981-9893

© 2021 Marco Toral. All rights reserved.

No part of this book may be reproduced, stored in a retrieval system, or transmitted by any means without the written permission of the author.

Published by LitPrime Solutions   10/21/2021

ISBN: 978-1-955944-24-3(sc)
ISBN: 978-1-955944-25-0(hc)
ISBN: 978-1-955944-26-7(e)

Library of Congress Control Number: 2021922929

Any people depicted in stock imagery provided by iStock are models, and such images are being used for illustrative purposes only.

Certain stock imagery © iStock.

Because of the dynamic nature of the Internet, any web addresses or links contained in this book may have changed since publication and may no longer be valid. The views expressed in this work are solely those of the author and do not necessarily reflect the views of the publisher, and the publisher hereby disclaims any responsibility for them.

CONTENTS

PART ONE: THE HIGH LIFE OF FREEDOM 1
Chapter 1. Born as an Ouano and being in a prominent family . . . 3
Chapter 2. A fledgling businessman 11
Chapter 3. Becoming a family man and my eventual downfall . . . 17
Chapter 4. Arrest and unraveling 19
Chapter 5. The lowest point 23

PART TWO 27
Chapter 6. Picking myself up 29
Chapter 7. The Philippine jail system 33
Chapter 8. Hurry up and wait, and wait 37
Chapter 9. The transfer and the appeal 41
Chapter 10. After seven years 59
Chapter 11. My son's point of view 69

PART THREE: NEVER LOSE HOPE 73
Chapter 12. Restart 75
Chapter 13. Making a Happy Jail 81
Chapter 14. Visitors and Gelo's help 85
Chapter 15. The pressure 91
Chapter 16. My new life 95
Chapter 17. My mother's poem 103

The High Life of Freedom
- Childhood /My memories of my parents/ Growing Up in an Influential clan
- Getting Married/ Having a newborn son/ Running several businesses

The Consequences of Bad Decisions
- How did i get involved in the Drug Trade
- The Arrest
- 7 years Behind Bars the lowest points of my personal life
- Marriage annulled / missing my son/ mother's perseverance/ shame brought to the family

My name is Marco Toral and I'm a former inmate.

Honestly, it would be so much easier and simpler to just paint my life with that simple brush--that I did bad things and made wrong decisions that landed me in jail--but now that I have the chance to look back on my life, I realized that no life is ever simple, especially not mine.

I was in jail for seven years for drug possession and those were the darkest moments of my life but in the same way, that experience taught me a lot of things about life. About how your past need not define you and you can do a lot of things to turn things over as long as you don't lose hope.

Spending seven years in jail is not easy but what carried me through was hope, hope that one day, when I come out, I'll be able to make amends and I'll be able to turn my life around. And it did as in a funny twist of fate, I saw myself--a free man--going back to the jail of Cebu City not as an inmate but as a consultant doing my best to create a better situation for the inmates just as I once was.

But before I talk more about that, it's good to know how I got there, especially since my life was normal until my bad choices upended everything.

PART ONE

THE HIGH LIFE OF FREEDOM

CHAPTER 1

Born as an Ouano and being in a prominent family

I'm Marco Toral, the eldest of two sons of Edna Ouano Toral and Miguel Gamos Toral, born on the 6th of March 1965. I am also the eldest grandchild of my maternal grandfather, Ernesto C. Ouano, Sr., the patriarch of our side of the Ouano clan.

If you're a native Cebuano, you'd know the name Ouano. We are a prominent family of politicians and businessmen. I come from the latter and from a young age, and as the eldest grandchild, my grandfather has always been keen on making me learn the ropes of our many businesses.

One of my most vivid memories of my grandfather was him making his grandchildren, especially me because I'm the eldest, work in the salt beds every summer in high school. I worked in our salt beds, sweeping the salt after it dried and bringing it to the warehouse after that. He made us do hard work because my grandfather was very patriarchal in his way of management and wanted us to learn to run the businesses on his own terms.

At this time, my grandfather was busy building the Ouano Reclamation Area and the Ouano Wharf in Mandaue City. The family also operated a ferry service to and from Mactan Island and I was also taught to operate the barge at a young age.

The Ouano Wharf in Mandaue City is one of the busiest wharves in the country and is home to new ships bought from other countries like Japan, Korea, and China and started operations in the 1970s.

My grandfather's first business which served as the backbone of our family and led us to develop into other areas was in salt and my grandfather owned huge tracts of land he used to manufacture salt, but when the opportunity arose to turn it into something more profitable, the land was later converted to an industrial zone. This zone is the industrial hub of Region VII and is home to about 10,000 industrial and commercial companies including some of the biggest companies in the country such as San Miguel Corporation and Coca-Cola Beverages Philippines.

Looking back, I would attribute not being afraid of doing hard work from my grandfather, and in a way, I consider it his way of teaching us and building our characters, by making us do jobs that require particular skills and time to prepare us to handle the family business which was largely about leasing real estate. Basically, I grew up learning the ropes of our businesses in preparation to handle some of them when I grow up and this included knowing how to concrete roads and doing payroll. We also planted grapes and made table wine we sold.

As an Ouano, I'd admit that I lived a pretty comfortable life and I'd like to thank my mother for that. In fact, I'd like to thank my mother for everything as she has been the single biggest factor in my life.

An early photo of me with my mother, Edna

I was much closer to my mother than my father, while my brother Anthony was the opposite, he was closer to our father.

Our family was pretty normal until my father became an alcoholic. My father and I were close and he was a good father but his drinking problem resulted in problems in my family that eventually led to him leaving us when I was 15 years old. He returned to our family at 22 but he once again left, this time for good.

When I think about my father, I'd like to remember him as a hardworking man and despite all his faults, I'd like to think he was a good man who made bad decisions. He ran his own business though he did work during the reclamation of the Ouano Wharf in the late 1960s.

Our relationship eventually fell apart because of his alcohol abuse and while I like to think of our better days, looking back, our family problems have played a big part in the decisions I made down the line and I'm not proud of that but I have accepted it as part of who I have become. My father passed away in 2008, at the age of 69, due to complications caused by his alcoholism.

My family and I used to go to zoos and do other recreational activities

Eating out at the Sky-vue Revolving Restaurant in Cebu City

My mother is a very religious person, she's a devotee of Our Lady of Manaoag and at a very young age instilled in us good values and the importance of acceptance, love, and hope, lessons that I only completely understood when I was lying on the floor, sharing a cell with 25 other inmates in Mandaue City Jail.

Ouano Wharf in 1975

The Ouano building in Mandaue, Cebu

Ouano wharf in 2021

Ships docked at Ouano Wharf

CHAPTER 2

A fledgling businessman

Growing up, I looked up to my grandfather and wanted to become like him--a big-time businessman and visionary--and my studies reflected that goal. I went to the University of San Carlos in high school and after graduating, I left for the United States to join the International Study Tours in San Diego, California where we lived with an American foster family for two months to learn how they live.

Afterward, I traveled to San Francisco wanting to take a business management course at the University of San Francisco but since I didn't have a student visa, I had to come home to the Philippines to finish college.

When I was in San Francisco

I took the University of the Philippine College Admission Test (UPCAT), which was--and until now--considered to be the hardest college entrance examination, and that passing it meant that you will be able to attend the most prestigious school in the country. While waiting for my result, I enrolled in an electronic and communication engineering course at the University of San Carlos-Talamban campus.

A few weeks passed, and the results of the UPCAT came out, and I passed, so I withdrew from my course at the University of San Carlos and enrolled in UP-Cebu, and took up a business management course. I graduated in 1986.

At the time, because I liked my experience in the United States and I strongly felt that I could build my own life there, I left for the U.S. after getting my degree in 1986.

I was 21 years old when I went to the U.S. and decided to work a few blue-collar jobs to get me started: I worked double shifts at McDonald's and Pioneer Chicken in Oceanside, California, and then flew to Dallas, Texas to join a college buddy who was working in the Dallas Fort Worth area. I worked in one of the biggest malls in Dallas Valley View Center as a janitor, a warehouseman, a cook, and some other jobs.

It was tiring work but at the time I felt like I was living a carefree life while I worked towards fulfilling my dreams.

A few months later, my mom came to visit and told me about my grandfather wanting me to come home because he wanted to enter the ice-making industry and wanted me to manage his new company.

And because of how much I idolized my grandfather, I saw this as an opportunity to not only prove myself but also carve out a future for myself, so I went home.

I went home with such excitement and fervor that everything came to a grinding halt when I realized that instead of managing an already established business, my grandfather wanted me to build it from the ground up. I had to learn how to run an ice-making facility on my own.

It was hard work, a trial by fire, and until now I remember the rocky first few years of running the business and how much I learned along the way.

One of the things I learned from my grandfather aside from hard work, is to learn how to paddle your own canoe, which meant not depending on anyone else and taking ownership and responsibility for your decisions. He also taught me to be kind to everyone and that a good businessman should know the price of the drippings of salted fish in the market, which meant knowing everything there is to know about your business and to continuously work and put in the time to grow it.

And for 15 years, I felt like I was doing something I was born to do--a businessman through and through.

Me, at 5 years old, with my grandparents

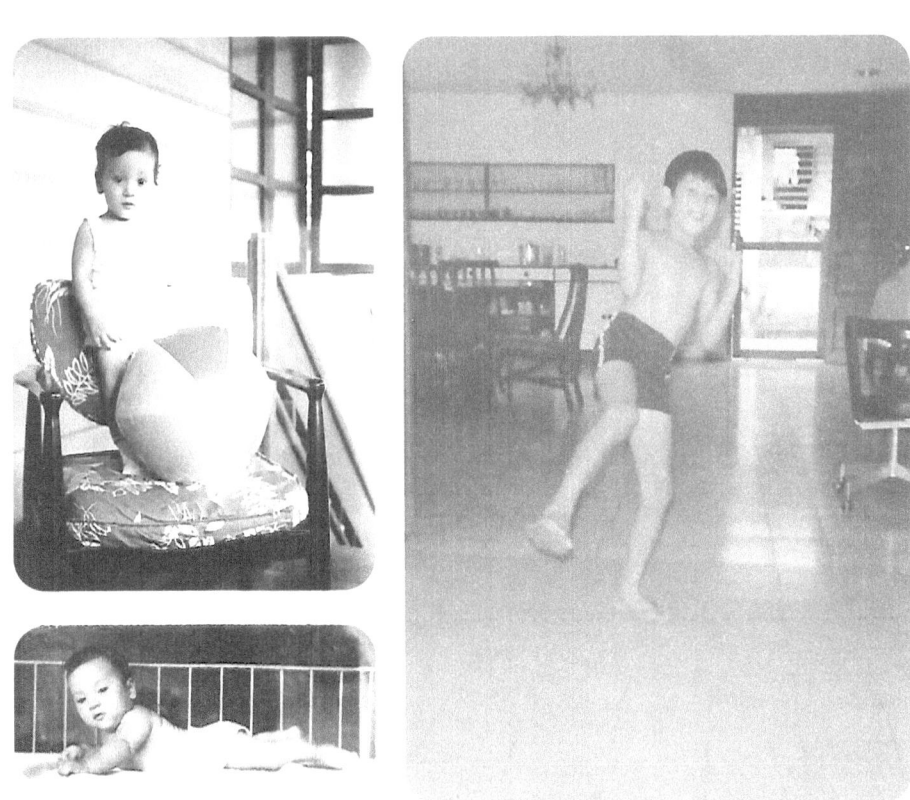

Some photos of me growing up

CHAPTER 3

Becoming a family man and my eventual downfall

I met my first wife during my second year of college and she was a freshman. She has always been very soft-spoken and formal. After seven years of courtship, we married and eventually bore a son, Marco Angelo.

Our family was close and we used to go and hear mass every Sunday. It was an idyllic life and if you're outside looking in, you'd assume that it was the makings of a perfect life: having a thriving business and a loving family, but everything was not as it seemed as underneath, I was already dabbling with drugs since I was 22 years old. And none of my family knew about it until 2002, when at 36 years old, I was caught in an entrapment operation and was sent to jail.

I could make a lot of excuses about why I started doing drugs: I was carefree, it was peer pressure because I ran with the wrong crowd, it was the pressure of running a business from scratch, it was because I still harbored resentment of being in a broken family, or maybe substance abuse ran in the family since my father was alcoholic. And it may very well be one or all of these things. Looking back, I guess I didn't even know why I did it, only that I did and it was my unraveling.

(My brother Anthony and I were polar opposites: I mostly kept to myself, was shy, and had a very small circle of friends. Anthony is very outgoing and has a huge circle of friends. But different as we were, we both struggled with drug use.)

But while I did use drugs, mostly marijuana and cough syrup, and meth, I would never consider myself a drug addict, I did drugs but was never addicted to it. It was something I used to take the edge off when stressed but I would function normally without it and that was how I kept that part of myself separate from the life people see for almost 15 years.

CHAPTER 4

Arrest and unraveling

It was a cool night on November 8, 2002 when a friend of mine asked me if I could supply her a large quantity of *shabu* (what meth is called in the Philippines). I told her I couldn't because I don't deal with that amount as I only ever use a small quantity for personal use.

I'm not a drug dealer, I told her. And she said okay, but can you meet me in the Mandaue Sports Complex to hang out. Agreeing to that meet-up was my downfall as I didn't know that it was going to be an entrapment operation, that she was working with the police to get me behind bars.

Maybe my friend became an agent so she could earn a lighter sentence and the exchange was to out the crowd she associates with and I was the sheep being led to slaughter. Whatever the reason was, she succeeded and I had to pay for the consequences of my decisions.

It was in 2002 when then-President Gloria Macapagal-Arroyo made into law Republic Act 9165 or the Dangerous Drugs Act of 2002. This new law was aimed towards safeguarding Filipinos, especially the youth, against harmful drugs by imposing higher punishments including life imprisonment for drug possession, importation, manufacture, and distribution. At the time, President Arroyo started her own anti-drug campaign after statistics showed in May 2002 that there were more than 1.8 million regular drug users and over 1.6 million occasional users.

The year 2002 and its succeeding years under the Arroyo administration, a large number of raids and arrests were made and the war against drugs became one of the primary missions of the Philippine National Police and the National Bureau of Investigation alongside terrorism and kidnapping.

So that November night I went to the complex together with my employee and we hung out but my instinct told me the moment I went to the complex that something wasn't right--there were too many cars. I saw a car parked a little bit farther from the car she was riding and there were people there.

When we met, she asked about her order and I told her again that I didn't bring anything other than what I use, so she dropped the subject and we hung out. When we left the place, right after we got out of the exit gate, all hell broke loose and several men surrounded me and pointed their guns at us. A small packet of *shabu* was found on my person and the police confiscated a firearm my employee brought and we spent the night at the NBI Headquarters in Capitol Site, Cebu City as we await to be charged.

At the time, spending my first night in a cell at the offices of the National Bureau of Investigation (NBI), I was confident that I would be spending a night in jail before maybe posting bail and getting out the next day. Never have I thought that I would be spending 31 days inside the NBI compound before being remanded to the Mandaue City Jail on December 10, 2002.

And the irony of ironies? The land upon which the Mandaue City Jail was owned by my grandfather which he then donated to the government.

I was charged with Section 5 of R.A. 9165 for selling drugs, which is a non-bailable offense, Section 11 for possession of drug paraphernalia, Section 15 for drug use, and R.A. 10591 for illegal possession of firearms.

According to my mother when she heard of my arrest, she initially thought I was kidnapped or something as my ex-wife told her that I was "taken" and it was not immediately clear to her that it meant "taken by the police" and not "taken" as in kidnapped. Her first thought was to immediately prepare the money for my ransom.

And when reality sunk in, she said that she couldn't believe it that I, her eldest and shy son, was arrested for drug charges. She was in denial until we met and I really was in prison, and even then, she said, she could not believe it.

(She said she would've believed it if it were my brother as he did have a history of substance abuse.)

Such was the life I led. I was a good family man and businessman who had a drug problem who managed to hide it from everyone for more than a decade and a half.

Many people are like me, functional drug users who often live unremarkable, normal lives. A recent survey by Addictions.com in 2017 showed that habits of drug users are mostly normal--they get an average eight-hour sleep, wake up, and go to work, you know, just like regular, everyday people. It's just that we're also keeping a secret drug.

It also took a few weeks for it to sink in, that I was going to jail and staying in it because I always held out hope that my case would be dismissed and I could go home and return to the life I had before.

But it didn't end up that way. Instead, as I spent sweltering nights lying on the floor with 25 other people, I realized that this was it, I really was in jail and it could be for a long time.

CHAPTER 5

The lowest point

Life in jail wasn't easy because it was rife with overcrowding, poor food, and poor facilities. Every day, we are required to wake up at 6 a.m. for the morning roll-call, then another roll-call at 2 p.m. and 10 p.m. then in-between we just sit around and do nothing.

I spent so many days doing nothing and feeling sorry for myself, missing my family, especially my son who was in sixth grade at that time that there were times when I thought about ending my life.

I entered the Mandaue City Jail in December and I remember it being the saddest Christmas of my life. Being part of a big clan and being Filipino, we put so much importance in spending Christmas and New Year's together and we always had so much fun and the best part was enjoying each other's company and bonding over good food. It was probably one of the very few times in the year where everyone can catch up with each other.

Since it was my first Christmas in jail, it was only my mom and two of my aunts who came to visit and I felt very depressed and lonely because

I couldn't even celebrate Christmas with my wife and son. Though I did celebrate with the other inmates--we had a potluck, a Christmas program, and I even joined a basketball tournament but nothing could lift my spirits up, as those only served as distractions.

That year, I spent it without my family, and I didn't know when I'll be able to spend it with them again.

Days went on and my mother, without fail, visited me every Saturday. And I looked forward to those days because she was the only link I had to my life outside. It was hard, seeing her struggle due to my situation, but I will always be thankful that she never left me.

She'd tell me that because she knew the jail had poor air circulation and I was having a hard time adjusting to the sweltering conditions, she'd feel so sorry for me and turn off her air conditioning at night.

"I thought that my son was suffering in jail and he's not used to the heat there and whenever I'd think about him sleeping in jail, I'd feel so sorry for him and wanted to share his burden–feel what he felt–that I won't use the aircon even when it's summer," my mother said.

She would always tell me not to lose hope, not to give up, and later on, when I asked why she kept telling me that, she admitted that she was also doing it to remind herself not to give up and not to lose hope.

"It was a cycle," she told me a few years down the line. "I'd lose hope, then I'll regain it, then something will happen--like your trial getting postponed--and I'll lose hope again. So as much as I needed to remind you not to lose hope, it was also a reminder to me," she said.

Many of our relatives felt it was shameful to have one of them in jail for drugs and would tell my mother not to visit me by going through the front door of the jail and instead go through a side door so other people won't notice that she's visiting an inmate. I could understand the shame but I still resented them for it.

All the while, I was missing my son Angelo, but my wife, at the time, would refuse to let me talk to him or even visit me. It felt like she was cutting me off her and our son's life and it was heartbreaking. It was like she was treating me like I was dead. I learned from my mother that she refused to even let my mother visit or take care of Angelo, something my mother resented her for.

I then had that sinking feeling that maybe--no one's waiting for me outside anymore.

Inside one of the toughest prisons in the world
- What i saw and experienced while inside the prison
- The condition of the jail
- The slow justice system
- Inmates condition

The chance of being free again
- The court verdict

Walking out of Prison and Walking in to mainstream society
- It's not easy walking in to society after jail time
- Restoring relationships with :
- my family/ my son/ community/ more importantly Myself

PART TWO

CHAPTER 6

Picking myself up

It took several weeks before I started to feel like I needed to do something productive. I was never used to idleness because I was a businessman and my grandfather raised me to always be on the go because time is gold. So one day, I decided to do something about myself--to keep me occupied. I called a close friend of mine who runs a rattan exporting business and asked if the inmates and I can help him with his business. We can sand your furniture, I said, and he agreed because it was labor-intensive work and he'd need all the help he can get.

I asked the warden if it's possible for the inmates and me to engage in a little livelihood program because I thought it would not only take our minds off the boredom and the desolation, it was also a way for us to have some kind of independence.

We were paid P1 per chair and the money everyone earned is then given to the *bosyo* or the head of the jail building--he collects the money and uses it to give an inmate transportation money when they are finally released because most of the inmates in jail have no money and no way of returning home. Some may not even have a family waiting for them. It was our way of sending them on their way safely with a wish that they can pick themselves up and rebuild their lives.

Aside from sanding rattan chairs, we also made candles and rosaries. Being able to once again work with my hands, made me feel a semblance of normality and gave me back a bit of control over my life.

The jail warden, Joe Moring, and I became close while I was inside the Mandaue City Jail. He treated me almost like his son and I admired him--he was a tough-talking, no-nonsense guy. And while he treated the jail like a military camp, he had a soft spot for the inmates and always listened to their stories. I told him mine and after he realized that I was struggling to cope inside the jail and was often depressed, he always found ways to cheer me up with stories and allow us to do our livelihood programs.

This compassion was especially helpful for me because, at the time, when I was in Mandaue City Jail, my grandfather became severely sick because of prostate cancer. My grandfather was my idol, and in a lot of ways, my rock, and knowing that he was sick and that I couldn't even take care of him broke my heart. What's even harder was that his house was only a few meters away from the jail. It was really so near yet so far.

My mother would tell me during her weekly visit that my grandfather wasn't doing well and yet he would ask about me "eight to ten times a day."

"He would ask me, 'where is Marco? Why is Marco not here? When will Marco visit me?'" my mother said. And she and my aunts would tell my grandfather that I was in Camiguin (my wife's hometown) doing some work or putting up a business. But still he'd always ask for me.

My grandfather is a very intelligent man and a very astute businessman so we knew that not much could get past him and I felt like, somehow, even my incarceration was something he knew instinctively.

One day, my mother visited me and told me that my grandfather had a dream.

"I dreamt Marco was in a very small house and he was stuck there and couldn't get out," my grandfather told my mother.

And in my gut I knew that my grandfather had an idea of where I was and it will always be my eternal regret that I was not able to see my grandfather again until he passed away on March 26, 2005

The man I sought to be for my whole life left without even me saying a proper goodbye or saying sorry and being forgiven for not living up to his expectations.

CHAPTER 7

The Philippine jail system

All over the world, jails in the Philippines are some of the most overcrowded. In fact, in 2018 we're the sixth-highest prison population in Asia with 215,000 people incarcerated across 933 prisons in the country.[1] Many of these prisons are overcrowded and often mismanaged.

I spent three and a half years in Mandaue City Jail while awaiting trial and many of the inmates were like me--we're not yet convicted nor handed our sentences, all of us are pre-trial detainees waiting for our cases to be heard in court.

(The World Prison Brief, a database for prison systems in the world pegged that 75.1% of incarcerations in the country are pre-trial inmates. This makes the Philippines the country with the highest number of pre-trial detainees in Southeast Asia and second highest in Asia.)

---

1. According the Borgen Project (https://borgenproject.org/philippines-incarceration-system/)

And getting a court date and actually getting a trial is a lot of waiting and many inmates remain in jail far longer than what the punishment for their crimes would've been if they were found guilty. I met several inmates whose charges would entail about seven or so years in prison but have been incarcerated for ten without their cases reaching resolution.

The main problem was there's about one court for 50,000 people. There are simply not enough courts for our needs. In the Philippines, there are only 2,000 courts nationwide that serve a population of a hundred million. If you compare this ratio with developed nations, it's clear we have an undermanned justice sector, according to a February 2017 Asean Today report.

Courts are overburdened with cases and are short on staff to process them all, the Philippine Statistics Authority noted that there's an annual caseload of more than one million or an average of 4,000 cases daily. This means, a judge would have an average annual average workload of 644 cases.

Looking at this insane and disheartening statistics and the lack of enough facilities to contain prisoners, it's no wonder the Philippines has, for decades, struggled with overcrowding.

And with a prison accommodating sometimes nine times the number of people it was built for as in the case of the Cebu City Jail, getting proper, humane treatment is hard.

Inmates are given three meals a day but the meals barely suffice. I remember breakfast was a piece of *longganisa* (cured sausage) and rice, then lunch was *monggo* soup (mung bean soup) and rice, and finally for dinner it's *sotanghon* soup (vermicelli noodles in soup). And the quality is always poor, I remember the soups tasting like water and not much at all. The inmates were always hungry.

Again, I was very fortunate because everyday my mother would have our helper send me my meals because she knew I was not used to prison food. Every Saturday I'd ask her for a dish I'd like to have and she'll have someone to cook it and send it to me. I ate well in prison and I shared whatever I had with the inmates. They were very happy being able to eat regular food and I was happy to be able to share what I had with them.

It was at this point, when I opened my eyes into the plight of the inmates, that I realized that many things should be done to make these people's lives better. I've always subscribed to the belief that people are innocent until proven guilty and that prisoners should be treated humanely when a significant number of detainees are actually innocent. And mostly, people deserve a chance to change, to redeem themselves.

Halden prison in Norway, was consistently named the most humane prison in the world. Every prisoner has enough space to live in as every apartment-style area only houses eight people at the maximum. It has workshop areas, flat-screen TVs in the rooms, game rooms, and workshop spaces. Inmates spend very little time inside their cells and are able to walk around, exercise, and even learn new skills.

It's a luxury by anyone's measure and while this is undoubtedly impossible to achieve in most places, especially in a third-world country like the Philippines, but it was evidence that treating people better would not only be beneficial for the prison system itself but will also benefit the individual.

I read in a 2012 The Guardian article that Halden prison, despite housing some of the most serious criminals, there are rarely, if ever, fights breaking out and that prisoner-on-prisoner assaults and inmate deaths are very low. Unlike in the Philippines where 5,200 inmates die within prison walls every year.

In jail, I had nothing productive to do until we did small livelihood programs, and I found out that it was not conducive for re-entering society. At its core, while jails are meant to separate offenders for the safety of the general populace, they should also be a place where inmates can learn how to reintegrate into society, be better people, and not become re-offenders.

Carlos Conde, a human rights watch researcher, once remarked that "corrupt and incompetent investigators and prosecutors, a judicial and court system clogged with too many cases, and too few judges to try them. These institutional pathologies result in unjust and prolonged detention."

The inability to post bail also adds a burden to the system. Many Filipino inmates are poor and unable to post bail while common crimes like drug possession do not allow for bail according to data from the Institute for Criminal Policy and Research.

A slow justice system combined with a mismanaged, overcrowded jail system that puts only the bare minimum for its inmates and barely, if at all, rehabilitation measures, it's no wonder that many prisoners become repeat offenders and that crime persists even inside those walls.

CHAPTER 8

Hurry up and wait, and wait

I mentioned how the justice system in the Philippines is excruciatingly slow, it was something I experienced firsthand as I was detained in Mandaue City Jail for three and a half years before I got convicted and sentenced.

Every court hearing was about eight months apart but even with that much lead time, trials can be postponed for various reasons: the judge has a previous commitment, some things are not ready, etc. It was frustrating, to say the least.

Whenever I had a court hearing scheduled, I tend to be excited and get up early, take a bath and wear the prison uniform hoping that during the hearing I would be acquitted and gain freedom. Then we are loaded up on vehicles that will transport us to the court.

It was a quiet ride because the tension was palpable and everyone was nervous. How can you not be, when this may be the day you either go free or go back to the same overcrowded cell.

Once in court, I would sit on the bench waiting for my case to be heard and often it took the whole day because it wasn't just one case being heard, it's several and you had to wait your turn. The wait was long and you could see how much toll it takes on the inmate, many of whom are represented by public defenders, and rely on them to explain the court procedure and legalese. I also saw how regular Filipinos do not know about their rights or the law or basic court procedures.

After all the cases had been heard for the day, all of us were again transported back to Mandaue City Jail and returned to the usual routine. And then we wait again for another court date. It felt that all of my years in jail were spent waiting, and waiting, and waiting.

Do you know how it feels to be constantly waiting? During my conversations with my fellow inmates, we vent our frustrations of not knowing what lies ahead and that creeping fear that this may be it--that we will be in jail for the rest of our lives.

Sometimes inmates go to court hearings just to get it over with: they were already in jail and if they were convicted, well, it wouldn't really make any difference, would it? They will just be transferred to another facility and it's the same old, same old.

But as with all things, everything will soon come to a head and I had my day in court and I was convicted on the Section 5 charge on selling drugs and was sentenced to *reclusion perpetua* or life imprisonment. This was on top of my other charges (illegal firearms, etc) for which I was also found guilty.

The world came crashing down on me at that point and it was my lowest point because I knew that despite my drug habit, I did not sell drugs, and yet because of that one night, I was judged to stay in jail for my entire life.

What compounded my sadness then was the surprise that my wife was annulling our marriage. It devastated me. I thought and I hoped she'd be with me and that together we'd see through this together. I knew I had a lot to make up for and I knew I broke her heart when she found out about my drug habit.

I even understood why she wouldn't let our son talk to me because jail is not really conducive to the growth of children, and Gelo was only about 12 years old at this point. It was sad that I wasn't able to see my son grow up but I knew this was for the best.

What I never counted on was her giving up on me when I haven't given up on our family. My mother was the first one to learn of the annulment because the clerk of court was someone she knew. When the clerk saw my mother, he told her that my wife just filed for an annulment. My mother was livid and informed me.

I cried so hard at the time, maybe more than I ever cried before. A part of me understood but a part of me was angry and sad. It was a dangerous concoction, you know? I thought she'd stand by me. I thought I'd have a family waiting for me. I thought I had someone--other than my mother--who believed that one day I'll be out and be normal again. I guess I thought I would be forgiven, especially by my family.

That mass of negativity eventually saw me trying to take my own life but thankfully, I was unsuccessful.

Life was something worth fighting for, I thought. And so I picked up my pieces and was even more dead set on regaining my freedom but now with only one goal in mind--to see my son and be a part of his life. I may not have been able to save my family but I refuse to give up on my son. I only hoped that he didn't give up on his father as well.

CHAPTER 9

The transfer and the appeal

After my life sentence was handed down, I fully expected to be transferred to the New Bilibid Prison in Muntinlupa City–845 kilometers away from my native Cebu.

The document that sealed my fate

Republic of the Philippines
COURT OF APPEALS
Cebu City

TWENTIETH (20th) DIVISION

PEOPLE OF THE PHILIPPINES, CA-G.R. CEB-CR-HC No. 00413
Plaintiff-Appellee,

Members:

-versus-

MARCO TORAL y OUANO and

Accused,

Promulgated:

MARCO   TORAL y OUANO,
Accused-Appellant.   July 30, 2009 10:20 AM

x --- x

D E C I S I O N

Before Us is an appeal from the Joint Judgment of the Regional Trial Court, Branch 28, Mandaue City (hereinafter referred to as RTC for brevity) which found accused-appellant guilty for violations of the Comprehensive Dangerous Drugs Act of 2002 (RA 9165).

On December 3, 2002, accused-appellant was charged in Crim. Case Nos. DU-9754 to DU-9756 with violations of Sections 5, 12 and 15, Article II of RA 9165, committed as follows:

> "That on or about the 5th day of November 2002, in Mandaue City, Philippines and within the jurisdiction of this Honorable Court, the above-named accused, conspiring and helping one another, with deliberate intent and without being authorized by law, and with the use of motor vehicle (delivery truck) bearing

---

* Acting Junior Member per Office Order No. 530-09-CMV dated April 2, 2009.

CA-GR CEB-CR-HC No. 00413
Decision
x-----------------------x

plate No. GWA-979 and a Nokia 5210 cellphone, did then and there, wilfully (sic), unlawfully, and feloniously sell, deliver and give away to another "shabu" or methamphetamine hydrochloride, a dangerous drug, with a weight of 0.2070 gram.

"CONTRARY TO LAW."

"That on or about the 5th day of November, 2002, in Mandaue City, Philippines, and within the jurisdiction of this Honorable Court, the above-named accused, with deliberate intent and without being authorized by law, did then and there wilfully (sic), unlawfully and feloniously possess and have in his control one (1) plastic totter (sic), a paraphernalia for the use of dangerous drug.

"CONTRARY TO LAW."

That on or about the 5th day of November, 2002, in the City of Mandaue, Philippines, and within the jurisdiction of this Honorable Court, the above-named accused, having been arrested for Violation of Sec. 5, (sic) Art. II of the RA 9165 was subjected to a confirmatory test and found positive for the use of methamphetamine, a dangerous drug.

"CONTRARY TO LAW."

In Crim. Case No. DU-9754 for the offense of selling shabu, accused-appellant was charged together with ▬▬▬▬.

The factual antecedents as established by the prosecution reveal that on November 5, 2002, the NBI organized a buy-bust operation against a certain ▬▬▬▬ pursuant to an authority granted by the NBI Regional Director. The buy-bust operation was the result of intelligence information gathered sometime in October 2002 from a confidential informant who tipped off the NBI that ▬▬▬▬ was allegedly engaged in illegal drugs. The buy-bust team consisted of Agent ▬▬▬▬ as team leader, and Agents ▬▬▬▬ and ▬▬▬▬ as back-up. Prior thereto, a pre-operation conference was held wherein ▬▬▬▬ a confidential informant, was designated as the poseur buyer and four (4) marked Php500 bills were included in the buy-bust money totaling Php100,000.

Around 6:30 that evening, ▓▓▓▓ informed the NBI Agents that the deal for the purchase of 100 grams of shabu worth Php100,000 would take place at the Caltex Station in the North Reclamation area. Consequently, the NBI agents strategically positioned themselves at the said gas station. However, the transaction never pushed through because ▓▓▓▓ changed the venue to the Ouano Wharf. Objecting to the new venue because it was a private wharf, Agent ▓▓▓▓ advised the poseur buyer that the negotiations be made instead at the Mandaue Sports Complex. The dealer agreed to such proposal, and the team thereafter went to the new location where a delivery truck subsequently arrived. After the female informant of the poseur buyer pointed out ▓▓▓▓ who had alighted from the said delivery truck, the negotiations commenced. But ▓▓▓▓ only agreed to deliver the 100 grams of shabu at his office inside the Ouano Wharf. When the poseur buyer protested, ▓▓▓▓ offered instead to sell a few grams of shabu as a trial transaction. The poseur buyer then handed over to the dealer one of the marked Php500 bills in exchange for one sachet of shabu given by the latter.

After the consummation of the sale, ▓▓▓▓ called Agent ▓▓▓▓ and informed the latter that the subject was in the departing delivery van. When Agent ▓▓▓▓ relayed this information to their team leader who was posted outside the Sports Complex, Agent ▓▓▓▓ then blocked the delivery truck and ordered the occupants to disembark. The driver of the vehicle was recognized as ▓▓▓▓ while the other occupant was later identified as ▓▓▓▓. The suspects were then arrested and informed of their constitutional rights. After a body search, the marked Php500 bill including a tooter was recovered from ▓▓▓▓ while a revolver with live ammunition was seized from ▓▓▓▓.

At the NBI office, the suspects were booked and fingerprinted and it was there that the Agents learned that the seller whom they knew as ▓▓▓▓ was actually accused-appellant ▓▓▓▓

y Ouano. Without the assistance of counsel, the two accused were then subjected to drug testing and violet light examination. While ▮▮▮ tested negative for shabu in his urine, accused-appellant tested positive.[1] Accused-appellant's hands also showed the presence of yellow fluorescent powder,[2] the same substance dusted on the marked money. Moreover, the laboratory examination of the plastic sachet purchased by the poseur buyer as well as the confiscated tooter was found to be positive for methamphetamine hydrochloride.[3] Subsequently, after being reminded by the NBI Regional Director about the requirement for an inventory under RA 9165, Agent ▮▮▮ on November 6, 2002, drafted a receipt of the seized items[4] which the accused signed.

In his defense, accused-appellant claimed that on the night in question, he and ▮▮▮ were taking their newly purchased delivery truck for a test drive. They stopped at the Sports Complex only to meet a lady friend of accused-appellant named ▮▮. ▮▮ had previously called accused-appellant and told him that she would be dropped off by her friends at the said Complex. When accused-appellant invited ▮▮ to ride with them back to the wharf, ▮▮ told him that she would just wait at the Sports Complex while accused-appellant will get his car at the wharf. After promising ▮▮ that he would return to fetch her, accused-appellant and ▮▮▮ then left the Sports Complex. But as they were leaving the area, they were suddenly stopped by armed persons who later arrested them.

At the NBI office, accused-appellant claimed that he was asked to hold up a Php500 bill and that his hands were then placed under a fluorescent light. He also alleged that there was no request for urine examination, and after he held the marked money, he was blindfolded, handcuffed and manhandled. Although he reported the abuse, the medico legal officer who examined him at the NBI Building declared that no bruises were found on his person.[5] Maintaining that he used no alias name such as ▮▮▮

---

[1] Record, Exhibit "F", p. 14.
[2] Id., Exhibit "G", p. 17.
[3] Id., Exhibit "H", p. 18.
[4] TSN, February 13, 2004, p. 5.
[5] TSN, September 20, 2004, pp. 6-15.

CA-GR CEB-CR-HC No. 00413
Decision
x-----------------------x

accused-appellant denied the NBI's allegation that he sold shabu and that the tooter was recovered from him. He further contended that the marked Php500 bill was planted evidence because the only money in his pocket at that time consisted only of a Php1000 bill and three Php100 bills.[6] Insisting on his innocence, accused-appellant claimed that he was merely the victim of a frame-up and vehemently denied the charges against him. To corroborate his story, co-accused ▮▮▮▮▮▮▮▮ substantiated accused-appellant's story on its material points.[7]

After the accused pleaded not guilty during arraignment, trial on the merits ensued. On September 15, 2005, the court *a quo* rendered a Joint Judgment convicting accused-appellant and acquitting ▮▮▮▮▮▮▮▮ in this wise:

> "WHEREFORE, this JOINT JUDGMENT is hereby rendered in DU-9754, finding only MARCO TORAL y OUANO guilty beyond reasonable doubt for the offense Sale and Delivery of Dangerous Drugs under Section 5, Article II of R.A. 9165. This court hereby sentences MARCO TORAL with the penalty of life imprisonment and a fine of P500,000.00 together with the accessory penalties under Section 35 thereof.
> "For lack of evidence to prove conspiracy with MARCO TORAL y OUANO, the accused ▮▮▮▮▮▮▮▮▮▮▮▮▮▮▮▮ is hereby acquitted. The court orders for his release unless he is being held for some other lawful cause.
> "In DU-9755, this court hereby finds MARCO TORAL y OUANO guilty beyond reasonable doubt for the offense of Possession of Paraphernalia for Dangerous Drugs under Section 12, Article II of R.A. 9165. Accordingly he is sentenced with the penalty of imprisonment of six months and one (1) day to four (4) years and a fine of Ten Thousand pesos only together with the accessory penalties under Section 35 of the Act.
> "The period of prevention detention by MARCO TORAL y OUANO at the Mandaue City Jail shall be given full credit.
> "In DU-9756, this court hereby renders judgment upon MARCO TORAL finding him guilty beyond reasonable doubt for the offense of Use of Dangerous Drugs under Section 15, Article II of R.A. 9165. Accordingly, the court imposes sentence upon him

---

[6] TSN, November 19, 2004, p. 6.
[7] TSN, July 26, 2004, pp. 6-12.

CA-GR CEB-CR-HC No. 00413
Decision
x----------------------x

consisting of six (6) months rehabilitation at the NBI-New Horizons managed by VSMMC at Candabong, Argao, Cebu, together with the accessory penalties of the law.

"The court directs for the immediate destruction of the pack of shabu or Exhibit "K" and the tooter or Exhibit "L".

"IT IS SO ORDERED."[8]

Since co-accused ▓▓▓▓▓▓▓▓ was acquitted by the RTC, only accused-appellant Marco Toral is challenging his conviction on appeal before Us. Accused-appellant raises a single error: that the trial court erred in convicting him despite the fact that his guilt was not proven beyond reasonable doubt. In support of his stance, accused-appellant questions the non-compliance by the NBI of the procedure outlined under Section 21 of RA 9165 regarding the custody of the confiscated drug-related items. Likewise, accused-appellant claims that by the NBI's failure to immediately mark the seized items at the scene of the crime, the prosecution was unable to establish the first link in the chain of custody.

The appeal is impressed with merit.

In criminal prosecutions, fundamental is the requirement that the elemental acts constituting the offense be established with moral certainty as this is the critical and only requisite to a finding of guilt. In prosecutions involving narcotics, the narcotic substance itself constitutes the *corpus delicti* of the offense and the fact of its existence is vital to sustain a judgment of conviction beyond reasonable doubt.[9] It is thus essential that the prohibited drug confiscated or recovered from the suspect is <u>the very same substance</u> offered in court as exhibit; and that <u>the identity of said drug be established with the same unwavering exactitude as that requisite to make a finding of guilt</u>.[10]

Reasonable safeguards are provided for in our drugs laws to protect the identity and integrity of narcotic substances and

---

[8] Record, pp. 363-364.
[9] *People vs. Obmiranis*, G.R. No. 181492, December 16, 2008 citing *People vs. Simbahon*, G.R. No. 148668, April 9, 2003, 401 SCRA 94 and *People v. Laxa*, G.R. No. 138501, July 20, 2001, 361 SCRA 622.
[10] *Sales vs. People*, G.R. No. 182296 April 7, 2009 citing *Mallillin vs. People*, G.R. No. 172953, April 30, 2008, 553 SCRA 619.

CA-GR CEB-CR-HC No. 00413
Decision
x----------------------x

dangerous drugs seized and/or recovered from drug offenders. Section 21, Article II of RA No. 9165 provides:

> "(1) The apprehending team having initial custody and control of the drugs shall, immediately after seizure and confiscation, *physically inventory and photograph* the same *in the presence of the accused or the person/s from whom such items were confiscated and/or seized, or his/her representative or counsel*, a representative from the media and the Department of Justice (DOJ), and any elected public official who shall be required to sign the copies of the inventory and be given a copy thereof;" (italics and underscoring supplied)

These requirements are also found in Section 2 of its implementing rules as well as in Section 2 of the Dangerous Drugs Board Regulation No. 1, series of 2002.[11]

However, in the case at bar, it is patent from the records that the NBI never implemented the abovementioned procedure. Neither was it demonstrated that the NBI agents extended reasonable efforts to comply with the said requirements. No physical inventory or photograph was taken immediately after the seizure of the confiscated items, despite the clear and mandatory directive under Section 21. There is also no showing that the persons cited under the said Section were present at that time. Apparently, none of the statutory safeguards were observed. As testified by ▓▓▓▓▓▓ himself:

> "Q: Was this section (Section 21) followed by your office?
> A: It's a new law at that time, sir.
> Q: My question is was this followed?
> A: We did conduct an inventory but regarding that particular section, we did not follow?
> Q: So, not followed?
> A: we did not."[12]

In *People vs. Magat,* the Honorable Supreme Court pronounced that the *corpus delicti* was not proven, after it was found that the

---
[11] *People vs. Obmiranis, supra.* note 9.
[12] TSN, March 28, 2003, p. 25.

CA-GR CEB-CR-HC No. 00413
Decision
x-----------------------x

police officers did not comply with the procedure under Section 21 of RA 9165 and that the marking of the confiscated drugs was not done in the presence of the accused immediately after the seizure of the same.[13] In *People vs. Dela Cruz,* the Honorable Supreme Court also observed that the procedure under Section 21 was not followed and that the apprehending officer failed to mark the drugs immediately after the accused's arrest.[14] Consequently, the Supreme Court therein decided that the *corpus delicti* was not duly established and acquitted the accused. Likewise, acquittal on reasonable doubt was the pronouncement in *People vs. Sanchez* after it was found that there was non-observance of the requirements under Section 21 and that gaps existed in the chain of custody of the seized drugs.[15] Similar findings were detected in *Sales vs. People,*[16] *People vs. De La Cruz,*[17] and *Bondad vs. People,*[18] which ultimately resulted in the acquittal of the accused.

Although it has been ruled that non-compliance with Section 21 is not fatal as long as there is justifiable ground therefor, and as long as the integrity and the evidentiary value of the confiscated/seized items are properly preserved,[19] the Court is nevertheless disinclined to excuse the procedural lapses in the present case. Apart from the fact that no sufficient explanation was given for the procedural omission, nagging qualms also exist in Our minds which ultimately call into question the identity and reliability of the confiscated drugs and drug paraphernalia.

When asked whether the NBI followed the procedure under Section 21, Agent ▆▆▆▆ said that RA 9165 was "a new law at that time" to justify their non-compliance with the said provision. This is certainly a tenuous argument because as NBI agents responsible for the proper apprehension of offenders, they are presumed to know the law. On this point, it may not also be amiss to state the

---

[13] *People vs. Magat,* G.R. No. 179939, September 29, 2008.
[14] *People vs. Dela Cruz,* G.R. No. 181545, October 8, 2008.
[15] *People vs. Sanchez,* G.R. No. 175832, October 15, 2008.
[16] *Supra.* note 10.
[17] G.R. No. 177222, October 29, 2008.
[18] G.R. No. 173804, December 10, 2008.
[19] *People vs. Pringas,* G.R. No. 175928, August 31, 2007.

elementary rule that ignorance of the law excuses no one from compliance therewith.[20] Moreover, even before the effectivity of RA 9165, certain safeguards were already in place with respect to the proper procedure in the custody of confiscated dangerous drugs, which was not unlike the requirements in Section 21. *People vs. Magat* declared that prior to RA 9165, the Honorable Supreme Court applied the procedure required by Dangerous Drugs Board Regulation No. 3, Series of 1979 amending Board Regulation No. 7, Series of 1974 which obliged "any apprehending team having initial custody and control of said drugs and/or paraphernalia, [to] immediately after seizure or confiscation, have the same physically inventoried and photographed in the presence of the accused, if there be any, and/or his representative."[21] Based on the aforesaid Board Regulation, it is clear that the procedure stated therein is essentially the same as that required under Section 21 specifically on the necessity of the inventory and photograph of the seized items. The failure, therefore, of the NBI in this case to follow the procedure mandated under Section 21 of RA 9165 is manifestly unjustified.

Even if Agent ▬▬▬ claims that he made an inventory marked as Exhibit "I", this document is still worthless because it is constitutionally infirm. Significantly, Exhibit "I"[22] reads:

> "This is to certify that the following items were recovered in my possession by the NBI Agents on November 5, 2002:
> 1. Totter, (sic) shabu paraphernalia one (1) piece only.
> 2. P500 piso bill, marked peso bill, one (1) piece only.
> 3. Nokia Cellphone 5210 with SIM pack, one (1) unit only.

---

[20] Article 3, New Civil Code.
[21] *People vs. Magat, supra.* note 13, citing Board Regulation No. 3, S. 1979 as amended by Board Regulation No. 2, S. 1990 as cited in *People vs. Kimura*, G.R. No. 130805, April 27, 2004, 428 SCRA 51, 69, which reads:
xxx   xxx   xxx
SEC. 1. All prohibited and regulated drugs, instruments, apparatuses and articles specially designed for the use thereof when unlawfully used or found in the possession of any person not authorized to have control and disposition of the same, or when found secreted or abandoned, shall be seized or confiscated by any national, provincial or local law enforcement agency. Any apprehending team having initial custody and control of said drugs and/or paraphernalia, should immediately after seizure or confiscation, have the same physically inventoried and photographed in the presence of the accused, if there be any, and/or his representative, who shall be required to sign the copies of the inventory and be given a copy thereof. Thereafter the seized drugs and paraphernalia shall be immediately brought to a properly equipped government laboratory for a qualitative and quantitative examination. xxx   xxx   xxx
[22] Record, p. 20.

CA-GR CEB-CR-HC No. 00413
Decision
x----------------------x

>   4. Canter Delivery truck, plate number GWA-979
>   x --- Nothing follows ---- /
>   All other items not on this list were returned to me by NBI
>   Agent ▓▓▓▓▓▓▓▓▓▓▓▓▓▓
>
>   Signed
>   MARCO TORAL y OUANO"

At first glance, Exhibit "I" appears to be an "inventory" as it lists down the items that were allegedly seized from the accused-appellant. But, a closer scrutiny of the said document will show that it is actually in the nature of an extrajudicial confession. Notice must be taken on the personal tenor of the document, wherein the accused-appellant basically admitted that the seized items were taken from his person. Being in the nature of an extrajudicial confession, Exhibit "I" should have been made with the assistance of counsel. Agent ▓▓▓▓▓▓ however testified that no lawyer assisted accused-appellant at the time he signed Exhibit "I".[23] The prosecution even admitted during pre-trial that accused-appellant was not aided by counsel while he was examined at the NBI.[24] It has been held that the signature of the accused-appellant on the Receipt of Property Seized is a declaration against his interest and a tacit admission of the crime charged, for mere unexplained possession of prohibited drugs is punished by law. The signature of the accused-appellant on the receipt is, therefore, tantamount to an uncounselled extra-judicial confession outlawed by the Bill of Rights (Sec. 12(i), Art. III, 1987 Constitution).[25] Consequently, since the defense seasonably objected to this evidence when the same was offered,[26] Exhibit "I" must be considered inadmissible against the accused-appellant.

Nonetheless, even assuming that Exhibit "I" is admissible as the inventory required under Section 21 of RA 9165, the Court is skeptical that the items listed therein are the very same items taken from the accused-appellant. It must be noted that Exhibit "I" was

---

[23] TSN, February 13, 2004, p. 11.
[24] Record, "Joint Pre-Trial Order," p. 64.
[25] *People vs. Bandin*, G.R. No. 104494, September 10, 1993 citing *People vs. Mauyao*, 207 SCRA 732 and *People vs. Turla*, 167 SCRA 278.
[26] Record, p. 199.

made on November 6, 2002 or a day after the arrest of the accused. Also, Exhibit "I" failed to identify the seized items by its specific markings, despite the existence of such markings on the said items. Thirdly and most importantly, nowhere in Exhibit "I" is the sachet of shabu listed as one of the items purportedly confiscated from accused-appellant. Such conspicuous absence of the sachet of shabu in the said inventory is certainly irregular, if not suspect. Agent ▓▓▓ tried to explain this discrepancy by saying that the shabu was then in the possession of the chemist when they made the inventory[27] which accounted for the absence of the shabu on the list. But considering the irreplaceable value of the shabu as a key piece of evidence, this feeble explanation of Agent ▓▓▓ only engenders more doubts in the mind of the Court with respect to the *corpus delicti*.

Moreover, the Court's misgivings are not allayed by the fact that the NBI failed to immediately mark the confiscated items at the scene of the crime. As testified by ▓▓▓ the pack of shabu (Exhibit "K") was marked by ▓▓▓ at the NBI office.[28] Regarding the seized tooter however, no testimony was provided as to the time when the said paraphernalia was marked. In truth, in this case, only ▓▓▓—an NBI asset and a civilian—testified regarding the time when the seized evidence was marked, while the NBI Agents who supposedly handled such evidence disturbingly did not. ▓▓▓ identified the tooter and the pack of shabu by the markings he allegedly made thereon[29] yet his testimony is completely bereft of any statement that would shed light on the circumstances surrounding the markings, as to when and where these were made.

It cannot be denied that the immediate marking of the evidence is vital to the prosecution's case because uncertainties might surface later on regarding the identity of the seized evidence, thereby negating the existence of the *corpus delicti*. It has been held that where the buy-bust team failed to mark the confiscated

---

[27] TSN, February 13, 2004, p. 5.
[28] TSN, August 15, 2003, p. 23.
[29] TSN, February 13, 2004, pp. 2-5.

CA-GR CEB-CR-HC No. 00413 Page 12
Decision
x----------------------x

marijuana immediately after the apprehension of the accused, such deviation from the standard procedure in anti-narcotics operations produced doubts as to the origins of the marijuana.[30] A similar ruling was made in *People vs. Kimura* where the Narcom operatives failed to place markings on the seized marijuana at the time the accused was arrested and to observe the procedure in the seizure and custody of the drug.[31] *People vs. Santos* likewise declared that the identity of the *corpus delicti* was not sufficiently established by the failure of the apprehending officers to mark or initial the sachets of shabu at the scene of the crime according to proper procedure.[32]

The prosecution cannot hide the aforementioned procedural discrepancies behind the presumption of regularity accorded to public officers. As held in *People vs. Lopez*, "the presumption of regularity is merely just that — a mere presumption disputable by contrary proof and which when challenged by the evidence cannot be regarded as binding truth. Suffice it to say that this presumption cannot preponderate over the presumption of innocence that prevails if not overthrown by proof beyond reasonable doubt." Besides, where irregularities exist in the performance of the police officers' duties—as in this case—this presumption is effectively destroyed.[33]

The Constitution mandates that an accused shall be presumed innocent until the contrary is proven beyond reasonable doubt. It is the burden of the prosecution to overcome such presumption of innocence by presenting the quantum of evidence required. Corollarily, the prosecution must rest on its own merits and must not rely on the weakness of the defense. In fact, if the prosecution fails to meet the required quantum of evidence, the defense may logically not even present evidence in its own behalf. In which case, the presumption of innocence shall prevail and hence, the accused shall be acquitted.[34]

---

[30] *People vs. Laxa*, 414 Phil. 156 (2001) as cited in *People vs. Orteza*, G.R. No. 173051, July 31, 2007.
[31] *People vs. Kimura, supra.* note 21 as cited in *People vs. Orteza, supra.*, note 30.
[32] *People vs. Santos*, G.R. No. 175593, October 17, 2007.
[33] *People vs. Mark Dela Cruz, supra.* note 14.
[34] *People vs. Orteza, supra.* note 30.

CA-GR CEB-CR-HC No. 00413
Decision
x-----------------------x

In view of the foregoing, the Court cannot help but entertain serious doubts in the case at bar on the existence of the *corpus delicti*, which is surely an indispensable element for a successful conviction. Hence, for violations of Section 5 (Sale and Delivery of Dangerous Drugs) and Section 12 (Possession of Drug Paraphernalia), the Court is constrained to acquit the accused-appellant on reasonable doubt. When moral certainty as to culpability hangs in the balance, acquittal on reasonable doubt inevitably becomes a matter of right.[35]

One final note: although this appeal of accused-appellant appears to assail his three (3) convictions, there is evidence to the contrary which implies otherwise. The records disclose that with respect to the specific conviction for violation of Section 15, Article II of RA 9165 (Use of Dangerous Drugs) in Criminal Case No. DU-9756, the imposed penalty of six (6) months rehabilitation has already been served by accused-appellant. Based on the letter from the City Jail Warden addressed to the court *a quo* dated April 17, 2006, the accused-appellant was transferred to the Center for the Ultimate Rehabilitation of Recovering Drug Dependents (CURREDD) on April 12, 2005 (sic) pursuant to the April 11, 2006 Order of the court *a quo*.[36] Considering that the rehabilitation was to last for six (6) months only, the rational conclusion is that this particular penalty has already been executed and fully served by accused-appellant. The records also show that on the date he filed his notice of appeal, the accused-appellant, through counsel, filed a Manifestation and Compliance wherein he prayed for the immediate issuance of a commitment order or any order for his immediate rehabilitation.[37] In view of this specific plea by appellant himself for the instant execution of his rehabilitation, We deem it proper to consider such prayer as an express renunciation of his appeal herein but only as to his particular conviction for the use of dangerous drugs in Criminal Case No. DU-9756.

---

[35] *People vs. Obmiranis, supra.* note 9 citing *Mallillin vs. People, supra.* note 10.
[36] Record, p. 407.
[37] *Id.*, p. 366.

CA-GR CEB-CR-HC No. 00413
Decision
x----------------------x

WHEREFORE, in view of the foregoing premises, the Joint Judgment of the Regional Trial Court of Mandaue City, Branch 28 in Criminal Case Nos. DU-9754-55 is REVERSED and SET ASIDE. Accused-appellant MARCO TORAL y OUANO is hereby ACQUITTED of the crimes charged on the ground of reasonable doubt and ordered immediately released from custody, unless he is being held for some other lawful cause.

SO ORDERED.

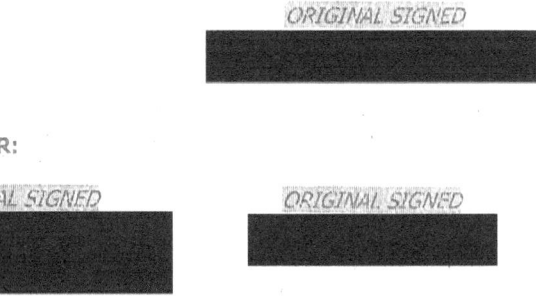

WE CONCUR:

CERTIFICATION

Pursuant to Article VIII, Section 13 of the Constitution, it is hereby certified that the conclusions in the above decision were reached in consultation before the case was assigned to the writer of the opinion of the Court (Sec. 5, Rule 8, RIRCA({a}).

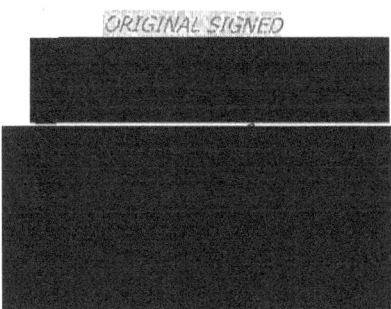

You see, when you're arrested and while awaiting trial and sentencing, inmates are detained in regional or city jails. We're not yet judged guilty or innocent, we're just people who have cases against us and are waiting for our day in court.

And once you've had your trial and pronounced guilty and handed your sentence, then from wherever jail you're staying in, you're going to be transferred to the national jail–Bilibid.

Bilibid prison is a nine-hectare facility that is the main insular penitentiary of the country. Designed to hold approximately 17,700 prisoners, its current prison population is at almost 29,000. Like many prisons in the country, it is overcrowded.

When I was incarcerated in Mandaue, it wasn't very comfortable but at least I'm with my people and my mother can continue visiting me. I'm still in my hometown. At that time, when I thought I was going to Muntinlupa, I was terrified–I knew very few people in Metro Manila and I've heard stories of gang wars inside Bilibid and stories of new inmates being given a hard time to teach them about the prison hierarchy.

I'm a timid and shy guy and while I did own guns and know how to use them, I'm someone who would prefer to solve things without violence. And I'd avoid trouble as much as I could. And I knew that being a new face in Bilibid, my safety may not be guaranteed.

I also heard rumblings that I may be transferred to Iwahig Prison and Penal Farm in Palawan–568 kilometers from Cebu. Unlike Bilibid, Iwahig is an open-air jail housing more than 3,000 convicts across 26,000 hectares. Convicts each take part in managing the arable land in the colony where they grow rice, corn, coconut trees, and various vegetables.

While hard work never fazed me, the fact that I will be in a place so far away from my family and maybe never seeing them again, was not something I wanted to do. But it's out of my hands now.

One day, my mother came to visit me while my transfer was being arranged and I admitted to her–and myself–that this may be the last time for a long time before I get to see her again.

"Don't lose hope, Marco. God will be with you. Trust in His plan," my mother told me. Again, this was one of the conversations we had when, looking back, was a message for herself as much as it is for me.

My mother's patron saint is Our Lady of Manaoag, a patroness for the sick, helpless, and the needy. While she was religious before, it was during my incarceration that she strengthened her fate. It was because she believed that God would not leave me behind, that He would see me through this challenge.

At Mandaue City Jail, the inmates and I would pray the rosary every 6 p.m. and I remember praying hard, harder than I've ever prayed before. I prayed to be granted freedom, the strength to see this all through, and most of all, forgiveness for my sins.

When a lifetime behind bars is staring you in the eyes, all I had in my hands at that time was hope, hope against hope that a miracle will happen.

My lawyer was trying to appeal my transfer to a drug rehabilitation facility in Cebu just so I don't have to go so far. He and his team looked at three rehabilitation centers and all those three rejected me because they feared that I would cause trouble and attempt to escape. No matter how my lawyers assured the facilities that I won't escape (and really, I won't) these centers didn't want to take the risk.

So my transfer seemed set in stone and I steeled myself and resigned myself to the possibility.

But then the director of the Cebu City Treatment and Rehabilitation Center (CCTRC) in Lahug, Cebu City agreed to take me in with the condition that I will be obedient, not try to escape, and turn my life around. I agreed in a heartbeat. And the judge mercifully allowed me to serve my time in CCTRC while I await my appeal.

As soon as I was allowed to appeal my case, I hired a very good lawyer to handle my case. I spent another three and a half years in rehabilitation. And time continued to flow outside my cell.

CHAPTER 10

After seven years

Despite being in rehabilitation, I barely needed to be helped when it came to fixing my drug problem because I already quit cold turkey ever since the night I was arrested.

It was a small blessing that I didn't go through withdrawals though I did experience several sleepless nights, but that can be chalked up to the anxieties of being in jail.

In CCTRC, we were treated so much better than in Mandaue City Jail. We had enough room to sleep and a bed to sleep in. The facilities were also not as crowded and we were allowed to do exercises, play basketball, and various other activities to keep us moving and to help with our recovery.

Unlike in the City Jail though, I had to pay about P100 per day for the food, medicine, the facility, the doctors, and nurses. The food was better and filling though we were still allowed to have people bring us food from outside. And we get regular visitors too.

Within the center, we were separated into three groups: the blue shirts, who, like me, are first timers; the red shirts who were there for a second time; and the black shirts who've been in the facility multiple times.

Each group is housed inside a big classroom-like room and us blue shirts were about 50 people in all.

But despite having a better situation, all I really wanted was to go home free. I really miss my son and at this point, he was already in high school and a teenager and yet, I know nothing about him growing up, and at such a crucial time, too.

I wondered if he was coping well in high school and what he thought of me, his father who is in jail. I feared that he'd be ashamed of me and maybe even hate me. I even wondered what he wanted to be when he grew up or if he already had decided on the course he'd take in college. It saddened me that I was not there during a considerable part of his life.

My appeal was rolling while I was waiting inside the rehabilitation center. For appeals, I didn't need to show up in court so at least it was easier for me but the waiting, as usual, was excruciating–whenever my lawyer would visit me to discuss the case, my heart will always be at my throat and would drop whenever he'd tell me that they're still working on the case.

One day, my lawyer paid me a visit. At this point, I was already three-and-a-half-years in the facility. I thought it was like a routine visit, an update, because my lawyer and I meet every week or so to talk about the case.

But on this day, I noticed he was holding a large envelope that's full of documents and after we sat down, he asked to see the director of the facility. The first thing I thought was that it wasn't going to be good news and mentally I was preparing myself for when I'll be told my appeal was denied.

Maybe the apprehension showed on my face because my lawyer smiled and said that everything's fine.

When the director came, my lawyer told him that I won my appeal and they needed to fix my paperwork for release.

It took a few seconds before what he said sank in and my lawyer had to repeat that **yes, I am going to be free. I won.**

I won. I won. I won. I'm free. I'm free. After seven years. I'm free.

Republic of the Philippines
COURT OF APPEALS
Cebu City

PEOPLE OF THE PHILIPPINES, Plaintiff-Appellee, -versus- MARCO TORAL y OUANO and ███████████ Accused, MARCO TORAL y OUANO, Accused-Appellant.	CA G.R. CR-HC. No. 00413 Criminal Case Nos. DU-9754 to DU 9756 RTC, Branch 28, Mandaue City

ENTRY OF JUDGMENT

This is to certify that on <u>30 July 2009</u> a Decision* rendered in the above-entitled case was filed in this Office, the dispositive part of which reads as follows:

x x x In view of this specific plea by appellant himself for the instant execution of his rehabilitation, We deem it proper to consider such prayer as an express renunciation of his appeal herein but only as to his particular conviction for the use of dangerous drugs in Criminal Case No. DU-9756.

"WHEREFORE, in view of the foregoing premises, the Joint Judgment of the Regional Trial Court of Mandaue City, Branch 28 in Criminal Case Nos. DU-9754-55 is REVERSED and SET ASIDE. Accused-appellant MARCO TORAL y OUANO is hereby ACQUITTED of the crimes charged on the ground of reasonable doubt and ordered immediately released from custody, unless he is being held for some other lawful cause.

SO ORDERED."

and that the same has, on <u>30 July 2009</u> become final and executory and is hereby recorded in the Book of Entries of Judgments.

Copy Furnished:

MR. MARCO TORAL y OUANO – reg. w/ r.c.
THE DIRECTOR – reg. w/ r.c.
Bureau of Corrections
1770 Muntinlupa City

OFFICE OF THE SOLICITOR GENERAL – reg. w/ r.c.
134 Amorsolo St., legaspi Village
1229 Makati City

CEBU

№ 0572

THE PEOPLE OF THE PHILIPPINES
Plaintiff-Appellee
VERSUS
MARCO TORAL y OUANO and ▇
▇ *Accused.*
~~MARCO TORAL y OUANO~~
Accused-Appellant

CA-G.R. CR No. CR HC No. 00413
No. DU 9754-56 of the Regional Trial
Court of Mandaue City, Branch 28

ORDER OF RELEASE

GREETINGS:

WHEREAS, on the 30th day of July, 199 2009 a decision was rendered in the above-entitled case, the dispositive part of which reads as follows:

WHEREFORE, in view of the foregoing premises, the Joint Judgment of the Regional Trial Court of Mandaue City, Branch 28 in Criminal Case Nos. DU-9754-55 is REVERSED and SET ASIDE. Accused-Appellant MARCO TORAL y OUANO is hereby AQUITTED of the crimes charged on the ground of reasonable doubt and ordered immediately released from custody, unless he is being held for some other lawful cause.

SO ORDERED.

NOW, THEREFORE, *you are hereby ordered to release immediately the* ▇ *accused-appellant* MARCO TORAL y OUANO *unless there is any cause for which he should continue to be detained, furnishing this Office with* ▇ *tificate of your proceedings.*

GIVEN by the ▇

Department of Health
VICENTE SOTTO MEMORIAL MEDICAL CENTER
CEBU CITY TREATMENT & REHABILITATION CENTER (CCTRC)
(Formerly PNP Cebu-CUREDD)
Camp General Arcadio E. Maxilom
Salinas Drive, Lahug, Cebu City

August 11, 2009

Presiding Judge, Regional Trial Court
7th Judicial Region
Branch 28, Mandaue City

Subject: MARCO OUANO TORAL
CRIM. CASE NO. DU-9754 to 56

Your Honor:

    This has reference to the above-named subject who was recommended for temporary release from confinement and to undergo 18 months of aftercare and follow-up services by ███████████████, psychologist on 21 September 2007. An order was issued by your Honorable court dated October 19, 2007 for the continued stay of the subject in this facility while undergoing aftercare and follow-up services to prevent security problems.

    Please be informed that the subject is now through with his eighteen (18) months aftercare and follow-up services program. During the entire phase of subject's aftercare and follow-up services, he was able to satisfy all the rules and regulations set by the center. He fully realized the ill effects and the dangers of abusing drugs. He is remorseful of all the wrongdoings he had done in the past. He is now physically and psychologically drug free.

    In view of the above observations, subject is respectfully recommended for final release.

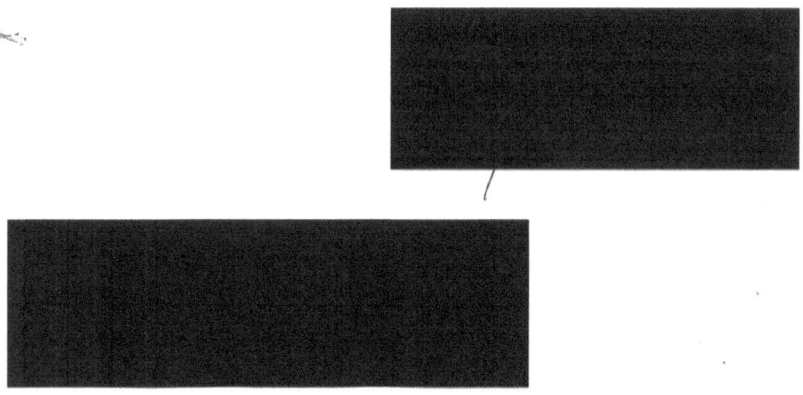

Me becoming a free man after seven years

I broke down. It was relief, it was happiness, and maybe it was also sadness. Seven years. Seven years of my life behind bars. Life as I knew it has changed and the people I knew moved on with my life.

"Congratulations Marco, you're free. I hope I won't see you coming back here again," the director told me. I can't remember if I answered him, such was my shock.

After a while I asked when I could be released.

"Well, after we handle your release papers and your payment for the facility, you'll be out of here in the afternoon," my lawyer said.

That day was August 8, 2009. The day Marco Toral was once again a free man.

It was late in the afternoon when we finished all my papers and paid the facility for my stay.

My lawyer brought me home to my mother's house. I called and knocked on the door and my mother went and opened the door.

At first she couldn't process what happened because my lawyer didn't inform anyone of my release. She thought she was dreaming.

"Ma, I'm home. I'm free," I told her and we hugged each other and we cried.

"My son is home. Marco is home," my mother told everyone.

My mother and I, as a free man once again

She then told me that she never stopped believing that I'll be free and now I'm here. It was such a joyous moment.

After we got ahold of ourselves, I immediately asked my mother about my son, Gelo, and she told me that my ex-wife brought him to Manila and that he's now in college taking a pre-law course at University of Asia and the Pacific.

I asked if it's possible to talk to Gelo and my mother said she'll call him.

I was afraid and yet expectant because I may be able to talk to my son, who I've never seen for seven years. I didn't know if he hated me or resented me because his mother and I are now separated and I didn't know how he'd react having a father who just came back from jail.

The phone rang for what seemed like forever then Gelo picked up.

"Hello, Gelo. This is your dad," I told him.

"Dad. How are you?" Gelo said over the phone.

My son's voice was deeper and I almost didn't recognize it but it brought so much joy to me that I'm talking to my son again.

I told him I was sorry for everything and that he shouldn't follow in my footsteps. I wasn't a good dad. I was just sorry for everything.

"It's okay dad. You're still my dad," Gelo said.

And I cried. I cried so hard. I was happy I finally reconnected with my son but I also mourned all the time that was lost. I mourned the people I lost and yet I felt happy that at least I had my son and my mother with me.

Me and my son, Gelo after we reunited

CHAPTER 11

My son's point of view

Gelo was in grade five, 11 years old, when I went to jail and before that, we had an idyllic life–I was running a successful ice-making business and other ventures and our family was complete and happy.

When I was arrested, my ex-wife chose to shelter Gelo from what I did. I knew she was disappointed with me and I understood, I was also disappointed with myself.

She never told Gelo that I was incarcerated on drug charges and my mother and the elders of the Ouano family who knew collectively decided not to tell him. It was best, they decided, that he lived a normal life.

A prison is not a good thing to expose a pre-teen to, and I agreed.

Gelo was an only child but he said growing up he never felt he was an only child because he always had his cousins from both sides of the family with him.

"I remember the Ouanos to be a happy bunch. They were always a joy to be around - especially during New Year's Eve in my Great Grandfather's house where everything was in abundance," he recalled.

And so life went on for Gelo who didn't know the real reason why his father wasn't there, he thought–like my grandfather–that I was away on business. He said he didn't remember if he asked my mother, who he calls "Mamalo" affectionately, or his mother what happened to me.

But it was obvious, he said, that something was wrong. It was apparent in the wave of sadness that blanketed the family, Mamalo and his mom. And still, he didn't have the courage to ask.

"And maybe, I was afraid to know what it was."

Eventually he learned of my arrest when one of his Ouano cousins jokingly told him that I was in jail because I'm an addict.

"I believed it, but I also immediately believed that whatever it was, it was temporary," Gelo said. "I knew and I know my dad as someone who always pulls through."

Knowing that this was how my son thought of me and that, like my mother, he had this unshakeable and unwavering faith in me that I'll get through this humbled me and I still get very emotional when I recall it.

When Gelo and I reunited in Manila, were both overjoyed that we can finally see and be with each other again in and relieved that there was finally certainty.

The actual reunion, despite that first emotional phone call, was very light and casual, almost as if nothing had happened.

"I remember him apologizing for what had happened, but I remember shrugging it off as something very minor and we continued on to bond over a meal and some drinks. I guess we both subconsciously decided to not let what happened affect us more than it already has and we just wanted to move on from it," Gelo remarked.

When we talked about what happened to our family, why my ex-wife and I had our marriage annulled, Gelo said that at the time, he was very disheartened because nobody wanted a broken family. But as he matured he understood his mom's decision and respected her greatly for it because it was a decision made with Gelo's best interests in mind. In the end, it was a decision born out of love.

What also touched me a lot was when Gelo told me that the reason why he wanted to be a lawyer was because he wanted to understand what happened to me and maybe he can help me.

"I think I was subconsciously drawn into it because of what was happening at that time. As I grew older, my interest in the law continued to grow and I was more curious about the different fields of law. It so happens that one of my close friends was in the same situation so ten years after my dad's incarceration, we enrolled ourselves into law school," he recalled.

I felt unworthy of his faith and love and resolved that I'll be the best father I know how to be and make up for those lost seven years.

All it takes for someone to believe in you
- My appointment at the Cebu Provincial Jail
- How did it change me and understand the plight of the inmates

PART 3
NEVER LOSE HOPE

CHAPTER 12

Restart

I was incarcerated for seven years and understandably, I was chomping at the bit to go on a vacation because I'm now a free man once again. I had so many places I wanted to go, and of course, I wanted to see Gelo.

So when my mother asked me what I wanted to do, I immediately told her that I wanted to go to Baguio. And so to Baguio we went.

We spent two weeks in the Summer Capital reconnecting and recollecting. I've never been as jubilant or as relaxed as I was. It finally sunk in that I was finally free, and it was a sweet, sweet victory.

(We also took a detour to Manaoag in Pangasinan so my mother can thank Our Lady of Manaoag for giving her strength and helping grant her wishes.)

So two weeks came and went and while I was sitting at our home in Cebu, I had to confront a reality that I didn't know what I wanted to do with my life now that I'm free. The ice-making facility closed down during my stint in jail and I felt like I didn't have a place anymore in my other businesses.

Again, life moved on without me, all while I was waiting to get back to the life I left behind.

It also hurt that because of my incarceration, my relationship with the family also changed—my aunts and cousins looked at me in askance and I would hear whispers about how I'm a drug addict and how I'm a bad person because I was in jail.

I turned from being the golden boy of the family to the black sheep, a prodigal son. Someone who has lost his place and maybe even unwanted. So I stayed inside our house, hiding because even I believed that I brought shame to the family.

I've experienced so much behind bars that insults often roll off my skin but having my own family treat me like my unsavory past defined everything about me, hurt.

It hurt so much that one day I decided to go to the mountains, far away from the disappointed stares and whispers, and carve a life where there's no one to judge me. God knows, I've judged myself far worse.

So I went into the mountains and worked on land my family owned. I became a farmer taking care of chickens, pigs, vegetables, and fruits. It felt good having something to do, it felt like I finally had a purpose.

As a man who grew up using his hands, doing nothing inside jail was not something I was used to. I'm used to hard work and being a farmer gave me that sense of getting back myself. For seven years when I lost myself, working on the land felt like finding that old friend back again.

And so I farmed for two years and I was reasonably happy. I'd go down once in a while to see my mother and talk to my son. But inside it felt like something was missing. I'd always find myself thinking about my days as an inmate, wondering if my friends were doing well while lamenting the fact that many of them are still waiting for their own freedoms.

I also thought about how the jail system in the country sucked and how the inmates deserved better treatment.

I felt like I had to do something but I didn't have the means to do so. Some of my friends inside sometimes contact me to ask about me and ask if I can help them find work and I do help whenever I can but I can't help everybody. It was disheartening.

Adjusting to the outside world when you've been used to a cramped, sweltering room was jarring and very difficult.

Then one day, John Cobar–a close friend of mine back in college–visited me and asked me if I'd join them in the gubernatorial campaign of Hilario "Junjun" Davide. I was initially not sold on the idea because I was not used to being with a lot of people and I knew what people thought of me but John insisted that being out-and-about would do me a world of good.

I mulled over the idea and I realized that since I knew Gov. Junjun and his wife and I'll be with people who I knew and my friends, there really is no better way to reintegrate and carve my place once again.

So for months we went on the campaign trail, doing a lot of meetings, a lot of conventions, going door-to-door, and asking people to vote for

Gov. Junjun. He was getting traction and as days went on and finally people went to the polls, we knew Gov. Junjun was going to win.

One day I was called to Gov. Junjun's office. I thought he was just going to thank me for my contribution to the campaign but then he asked me to work at the Cebu Detention and Rehabilitation Center (CPDRC) as the jail consultant.

I was baffled. "But why, sir?"

"Because you were one of them Marco, you know what needs to be done to improve the situation inside," Gov. Junjun told me.

I couldn't make a decision immediately and I asked John's opinion and he told me that there's no better person than I to solve the problems inside the jail.

"You're privy to life inside jail including unwritten rules among the detainees, to maintain order and to instil discipline among themselves. You know what activities and programs to implement to make the detainees productive and to keep them busy," he said.

Then he added that I already have the experience–I led the livelihood project in Mandaue City Jail which helped improve the condition of inmates.

Thinking about what John told me and Gov. Junjun's confidence in me, I felt like it was something I could do. I had been thinking about the dismal state of the jails and I thought that being a consultant would let me do something good.

This is it, I thought. This may just be the chance I was looking for.

And so I returned to Gov. Junjun and accepted his offer to manage the Cebu Provincial Jail. And on July 1, 2013, Marco Toral, former inmate, became the jail consultant of CPDRC.

Me as the jail consultant of CPDRC

CHAPTER 13

Making a Happy Jail

If you watch *Happy Jail*, a documentary by Michele Josue, on Netflix, you'd see how I used to run things at CPDRC and how despite overcrowding and the generally unkempt condition of the jail, I did try my very best to make it a happy jail.

Before I took the post as a jail consultant, it took a lot of thought and consideration about the things I wanted to do. And there were a lot of things I wanted to do.

And on the day I first stepped inside CPDRC was the moment I realized, with some trepidation, that I'll be trying to fix a behemoth.

Unlike the Mandaue City Jail, CPDRC is a huge detention facility, about 1.4 hectares and houses double its 1,500-person capacity. It was overcrowded and overrun by gangs and drugs and violence.

But I was determined to do something good and I was never one to back down from a challenge. So on my first day, I asked the jail warden and security officials to set up a long table in the middle of the quadrangle.

Then I told all the inmates to come up to the table and surrender all their guns, knives, weapons, and contraband.

Immediately I heard murmurs of surprise—they didn't think I knew that they had illegal items hidden in their cells. But why wouldn't I know? I spent three and a half years in a city jail and I knew how the system worked like the back of my hand.

The inmates formed a line and one-by-one laid their cards on the table, as did I. While the table was being filled and almost collapsing with the weight of their contraband, I promised them that I'll do what I can to improve their situations. I may not be able to give them freedom, but I won't let them feel they don't deserve to have hope or be treated like human beings.

Afterwards, I met with the *bosyo* or the leaders of the jail buildings. These are the people who keep the peace inside the jail and run it because security and the warden can only do so much. In a lot of ways, the *bosyos* are the ones that keep the jail from descending to complete anarchy.

"I'm one of you," I told them. I told them I was also an inmate, that I was out because I won my appeal. I believe that it was at that time that I earned a little bit of their respect because they knew I understood and that the change I'll be doing would be for the inmates' benefit. In the end, though, I knew that respect had to be earned, so I went to work.

In the next few days, I did thorough inspections of the buildings and I realized that CPDRC was completely decrepit and was not equipped to handle as many people as they are holding now.

It also was a funny facility, the watchtower was shorter than the facility walls and many places needed fixing, and I had to fix it.

I called all the inmates and had security personnel ask which ones were carpenters, builders, mechanics or handymen. I had them ask about each inmate's skills and once everyone was sorted by their occupations, I now had the workforce I needed to fix up the detention center.

I directed the carpenters and builders to fix leaky ceilings, broken walls, broken furniture, anything that needed fixing while I asked the mechanics to take apart the vehicles that were parked inside the facility and sell the parts for more funding.

Of course, this was not for free. I paid the workers P50 a day from my own pocket until we had the funding to pay the inmates for the job they're doing because hard work deserves proper compensation.

Basically, I created a livelihood program for the inmates and kept them productive because idle hands and feet lead to discontent and disorder.

I also supported the Cebu dancing inmates program. The program went viral in the latter part of the 2000's when their performance, dancing to Michael Jackson's "Thriller" was uploaded on YouTube and was watched by millions and millions of people all over the world.

The Cebu dancing inmates

I heard even the King of Pop himself saw the video and was pleased.

Allowing inmates to have activities that will not only keep them busy but also entertained became very beneficial for their mental health and I felt that they were happier with the way things are run. Dancing was their stress reliever.

CHAPTER 14

Visitors and Gelo's help

As an inmate who did nothing but sit around all day, the highlight of my day was when my mother and some friends would visit me. It made me feel like I've not been forgotten and that there are still people who care about me and are waiting for me to come home.

It was something I wanted the inmates at CPDRC to have because at the time, visits were very limited and that disheartened the inmates.

With the almost blanket authority given to me by Gov. Junjun, I opened the doors of the jail to visitors regularly so they could meet with their families, see their children, and their friends.

It was something I actually wanted to have while I was behind bars, the opportunity to see my family regularly. Maybe that's why I was so insistent on having regular visits.

Then I overhauled the facility menu, because the quality of food inside the facility was one of the things I knew needed changing. I remember having to eat bad food that mostly tasted like water and not much else but unlike other inmates then, I had my family bring me good food.

The inmates were always hungry because they were not fed well and I sought to change that so I ordered cafeteria staff to increase the number of meals with meat to three times a week and despite working on a small budget, the quality of food improved.

Inmates are human beings too and they deserve to be fed well, especially because the people within CPDRC are not yet convicts, they are people who are waiting for their trial dates. It was a detention facility, not a prison.

Many people within the facility, because of the slow justice system, spend way more time inside than what the punishment for crimes entailed. And some spend almost a lifetime behind bars waiting for a judge to decide whether they were guilty or innocent.

It was a very sad state of affairs and it was, again, something I wanted to change. I knew I was very fortunate because my family was well-off enough to get me good legal representation but most of the inmates don't even have money to hire private lawyers and have to rely on public defenders, who themselves are often overburdened with cases.

Knowing that my son Gelo was taking up law, I asked if he could come over and help out with some of the cases of the inmates and he readily agreed and even had some of his friends from law school to help out.

Gelo and I during his law school graduation

During one of our travels

Together with his friends, Gelo provided free legal advice service for inmates because they realized that there were very many unfortunate cases of inmates being jailed for far longer than the sentence had they been convicted; inmates not having access to any kind of legal advice; there were even some who had no idea why they were there.

"This problem is everywhere in our country, but since my Dad was the Consultant at that time for CPDRC, we saw it as a way to help at least one jail," Gelo recalled.

In *Happy Jail*, one of the inmates has been waiting three years for just a court date while another has been in jail for 15 years despite only having a four-year sentence if convicted.

Beyond legal services, I also instituted many programs including a sports program that allowed inmates to learn and play basketball, tennis, volleyball, badminton, and even boxing. I created the CPDRC SUPERMAX boxing team composed of 80 aspiring boxers.

Welcoming the 8-division world champion and boxing legend Manny Pacquiao during the launch of the CPDRC boxing team

We also set up infirmaries with doctors to take care of sick inmates, even bedridden ones. We also set up a bakery, an alternative learning system with the help of the Department of Education which helped few inmates graduate high school and elementary.

All of these were under my brainchild, the Inmate Welfare Development Program.

CHAPTER 15

The pressure

For three years as a jail consultant, no one could deny that I made definite inroads in improving the state of CPDRC. Morale was higher and the inmates were happier and there was less violence and discontent.

And it made me happy, but it was not without a lot of challenges. It took a lot out of me to keep doing what I was doing. I spent most of my time instituting reforms and making sure the programs were run efficiently, all while I was battling comments from government officials about the way I'm running the prison.

Governor Gwendolyn Garcia even said that the "jail was run by an ex-convict out on appeal" so how can it not be corrupt? I took offense with how she labeled me an ex-convict when winning an appeal meant that I was not a criminal. But that's neither here nor there.

She said that drugs proliferated within the walls of CPDRC when I knew that wasn't the case at all, we even had regular raids where the media would be with us and they saw that there were no drugs inside the jail.

It wasn't a dystopia they were making it out to be, in fact, it was a jail run by a former inmate who knew that jails and its inmates deserved better.

Because whenever I started programs and reform, I was not only giving the inmates better living conditions, I was also giving them hope. God knew that in those seven years, all that sustained me was hope and it was something I wanted the inmates to have.

I couldn't give them freedom, only the courts can do that, but I can give them hope and I can make their waiting a little bit more comfortable.

I had big plans, a lot of plans I wanted to do. I wanted CPDRC to be the jail that changed the jail system in the Philippines–the hallmark and the proof that the Philippines can do better in treating their inmates because even inmates deserve to be treated like humans.

But unfortunately, I was not able to do that. In 2016, an inmate escaped the facility which sparked so much criticism about the way the facility was run. I was told I was incompetent, that the programs were just window-dressing, that crime still festered underneath the surface.

And no matter how much I explained and fought for the job I did, it fell on deaf ears. The local government was determined to castigate me and the pressure became too much that I decided to resign.

The media thought I resigned because of the escaped inmate, it wasn't the case but it did contribute to my decision. Everything just became too much for me and it was better for me to step away from it all.

I remember thanking then-Gov. Junjun apologized for not staying longer but I left CPDRC with a clear conscience. I was proud of what I did and how much I did for the three years I was a consultant. I proved that change can be implemented and can be done effectively. It wasn't a perfect system, but I felt that what I did was a good start.

Sadly, everything I did was either discontinued or vilified. The visiting program was halted and even the much-loved dancing program was cancelled.

If you watch *Happy Jail*, my leaving left a dark cloud in its wake and the inmates were disappointed and some even felt that I abandoned them. I didn't want it to end this way but I felt that I really had no choice, all I could do was to assure them that I'll still be there for them though I'm not a consultant any more. I left CPDRC in 2016.

To this day, I still get phone calls from inmates asking me to come back, that it was so much better when I was there. Ultimately though, I believe that I did enough to prove my point and have left that part of my life behind.

I am Marco Toral, a semi-retired man.

CHAPTER 16

My new life

After leaving CDPRC, I am once again left without knowing what to do with my life but now that I am a bit older, I figured that I'll just enjoy my retirement. I lived a hard life and I felt I deserve taking it easy from now on.

So I spend my days fishing or on the shooting range. It was at the shooting range where I met my girlfriend, now my wife. We were target shooting in a firing range in Camp Lapu-Lapu.

Me at the firing range, a favorite hobby

Fishing with one of my close friends, Bernard

My wife Karen and I

She's young but she understands what I've been through and accepts me for who I am. I am at the stage of my life now where I am content and very happy and to explore my future with her. Right now, we are trying our best to make a family we can call our own.

My ex-wife and I also rebuilt our bridges, maybe time has a way of healing things and now we can talk civilly because in the end, we are still Gelo's parents and no matter where our life led us, we need to be there for our son.

My relationship with Gelo is going great, he was even my best man during my wedding. I feel very lucky to have a son who wants nothing but happiness, and I dearly wish the same for him. Gelo also recently married and I'm really happy for him.

Gelo and I during my wedding

I also started working at Cebu Arrastre as a de-facto supervisor. Cebu Arrastre is a company that offers manpower and stevedoring services for cargoes on Cebu ports. It's funny, if you think about it—I started working on ports, driving barges, and now I'm back at the ports. Life is a circle, isn't it?

When I was crafting this book, I was asked about how I wanted to be remembered as I have lived a very eventful life.

I thought about it for a long time and decided that I wanted to be remembered as a person who never lost hope, who realized that bad decisions do not make me a bad person, and that I was someone who tried to change the Philippine jail system.

And in the end, that's all that matters, right? That we do what we can, do what we know is right, and live life full of hope. I'm not proud

of everything I did in my life, but I'm proud of how I became who I am because of all my experiences.

I'm Marco Toral, a businessman, a former inmate, a former jail consultant, a family man, a father, a supervisor, and most of all, I'm me.

CHAPTER 17

My mother's poem

Through all of my struggles both in and out of jail, my mother has been my constant source of support and overflowing hope. I realized that no matter how hard life gets, a mother will always stand by your side.

And I feel that there's no better way to end my book with the poem my mother wrote for me while in jail in hopes that this brings you the same hope this afforded me in my darkest moments.

My mother and I

IN THIS LIFE
By Edna Toral

IT IS NOT WHAT THERE IS FOR THE EYES TO SEE
BUT THAT YOU BELIEVE

IT MATTERS NOT THAT ONE CAN SPEAK
BUT WHAT IS SPOKEN ABOUT

IT IS NOT THAT A HEART POSSESS
BUT HOW MUCH THIS HEART CAN FEEL

NO MATTER HOW LITTLE YOU HAVE
THE HAND THAT REACHES OUT
OVERFLOWS WITH LOVE

IT IS NOT HOW MANY A TEAR
BUT WHAT MADE YOU CRY
FOR TRUE FEELINGS THEY MAY NOT BE
AS ONE BY ONE THEY DIE

IT IS NOT HOW HEAVY THE SUFFERING
BUT HOW YOU BEAR THEM

IT IS NOT HOW MANY TIMES LIFE
COULD SEEM IMPOSSIBLE
BUT IF ONLY YOU KEEP HOPING

IT IS NOT HOW MANY TIMES THE PRAYING
BUT HOW YOU MEAN THEM

IT IS NOT HOW SAINTLY OR SINFUL YOU ARE
BUT WHAT MADE YOU BECOME

IT IS NOT THE LEGION OF FRIENDS YOU COLLECT
BUT HOW ONLY A FEW CAN BE TRUE TO YOU
TILL THE END

END

www.ingramcontent.com/pod-product-compliance
Lightning Source LLC
Chambersburg PA
CBHW021428070526
44577CB00001B/119